—SCIENCE—
THROUGH THE
—SEASONS—

WINTER
IN THE WOOD

—SCIENCE—
THROUGH THE
—SEASONS—

WINTER
IN THE WOOD

Janet Fitzgerald

Evans Brothers Limited

Published by Evans Brothers Limited
2A Portman Mansions
Chiltern Street
London W1M 1LE

First published in Great Britain in 1987 by
Hamish Hamilton Children's Books

First published 1987
Reprinted 1992, 1994

Printed in Spain by GRAFO, S.A. - Bilbao

ISBN 0 237 60215 6

Author's note

Books in this series are intended for use by young children actively engaged in exploring the environment in the company of a teacher or parent. Many lifelong interests are formed at this early age, and a caring attitude towards plants, animals and resources can be nurtured to become a mature concern for conservation in general.

The basis for all scientific investigation rests on the ability to observe closely and to ask questions. These books aim to increase a child's awareness so that he or she learns to make accurate observations. First-hand experience is encouraged and simple investigations of observations are suggested. The child will suggest many more! The aim is to give children a broad base of experience and 'memories' on which to build for the future.

The books in this series meet the requirements of the National Curriculum for Science at Key Stage 1 and 2.

The extension activities are wide and challenging and would adequately prepare children for work within Key Stage Two.

The books support scientific investigation in AT1 by encouraging children to:
• ask questions
• observe, compare and measure
• interpret observations

Through real life situations children are encouraged to sort, group and describe materials and events in their immediate environment. Questions are suggested and ideas presented which lead to predictions based on everyday experiences, which can be tested. The tasks encourage the children to go beyond a description of what they observe and to give a simple explanation of how and why it happened.

For AT2 the material supports the study of plants and animals in a variety of local environments.

Contents

It is Winter in the wood and
snow falls softly.

Snow makes a cover for all things in the wood.

Can you still see the shape of things?

What is underneath the snow?

Collect some boxes, plastic pots
and containers. Put them outside
when it is snowing.

Watch how the snow falls on
the boxes, pots and containers.

Has the snow filled them all to
the top?

What has happened round the outside?

It is Winter in the wood and
frost covers the branches.

What colour is the frost?

Can you see the pattern of the branches more clearly?

How does frost feel when you touch it?

One frosty morning, find a
twig and some fallen leaves outside.

Look closely at the frost.
Breathe on it to see if it changes.

What happens to the frost?

Are the patterns the same on the
twig and the leaves?

**It is Winter in the wood and
you can clearly see the bark on trees.**

What colours can you see in the bark?

Which bark has the most colours?

Which bark looks smooth, and
which looks rough?

Choose two trees, one with rough bark,
and one with smooth.

Make rubbings of the barks with paper
and crayons.

Can you see a difference between
your rubbings?

It is Winter in the wood and wind blows through the trees.

What has happened to the leaves from the trees?

Does the wind make a noise in the trees?

Can you make the sound of the wind?

Collect some straws of different lengths.

Blow down each of the straws.

Can you hear the sound of the wind?

Make a few holes in the straws.

Blow again. Is there a different noise now?

It is Winter in the wood and
some animals are asleep.

Look at the place where this dormouse has chosen to sleep.

What has the dormouse collected to make itself cosy?

Other animals just stay in
their nests when the weather is
very cold.

Sometimes they have to come out
to find food.

What do you think this squirrel
is eating?

It is Winter in the wood and there are tracks in the snow.

All kinds of animals make tracks in the snow.

This track was made by a rabbit.

Where will the rabbit look for food?

Go for a walk outside after
it has been snowing.

Look at the tracks made by your shoes.

Can you tell which tracks are yours?

How can you tell?

Look for different tracks.

It is Winter in the wood and
plants slowly begin to grow.

As the days get longer, some plants and seedlings begin to grow towards the light.

This is a beech seedling.

Look outside for signs of plants pushing through the soil.

You can grow some seeds indoors.

Try planting sunflower seeds
or marrow seeds.

Half fill each pot with compost.

Sprinkle a few seeds on top.

Cover the seeds with a little
more compost. Water gently.

Put each pot in a different place
and watch how the seeds grow.

It is Winter in the wood and
logs are rotting.

Logs are often wet throughout
the Winter.

Sunshine would help to dry them.

Is there much sunshine in Winter?

Find a log with bark.

Use a lens to look closely at the bark.

Can you see anything growing on the bark?

How does the bark feel?

What smell does it have?

**It is Winter in the wood and, if
you are lucky, you may see a fox.**

Where will the fox search for food?

If it is very hungry, it may leave
the wood to look for food in a town.

Many animals need to search for food in Winter. How can you help them?

Try giving different foods to the birds.

Which food do they like best?

Do they all like the same food?

Which birds like nuts?

It is Winter in the wood and
the deer are feeding.

The deer like to eat twigs
and the shoots of young trees.

They are in their Winter coats.

What colours can you see in their coats?

Look at the marks and patterns.

The colours will be brighter
in the Spring.

Look for signs of other animals
in a wood.

These cones have been nibbled by
a squirrel.

Find a cone and feel it all over.

Try to break off a piece of the cone.

For teachers and parents

We all recognise that children possess an insatiable curiosity about the rich environment and exciting experiences around them. For this reason they have a natural affinity for science and a basic inclination to explore and discover the world in which we live. We need to foster this sense of wonder by encouraging a scientific way of thinking in the early years. Children's own experience of the immediate environment will provide a natural starting point.

Through science children can evolve an active process of enquiry. This begins with observation (including sorting, comparing, ordering and measuring) and continues with asking questions, devising practical investigations, predicting outcomes, controlling variables, noting results, and perhaps modifying the original question in the light of discovery. The books in this series offer suggestions for engaging young children in this sort of active enquiry by relating seasonal change to familiar surroundings.

Extension activities

pp. 6–7
Encourage children to observe and investigate how snow falls. Does it fall straight down? Are all the snowflakes the same size? What happens to the snowflakes when they land on different surfaces? Notice how the snow settles, and if it makes a completely flat landscape. Try to discover what causes snow to collect in certain places, and to drift. Collect some snow and divide it into equal amounts. Place each amount in a container, and distribute the containers around the school or house. Note the melting time in each place. What is left when the snow melts?

pp. 8–9
Emphasise the crystalline nature of frost. It looks and feels different from snow. Look at the ice on puddles, and the frost patterns on ice and windows. Look at plants which have been affected by frost. Notice what has happened to them. Encourage observation of the way in which some plants have adapted in order to survive in frosts.

26

pp. 10–11

Look closely at the surface of bark for evidence of insect or animal damage. It may be possible to remove a small piece of bark from a log and find insect channels or spider egg sacs underneath. Always replace the bark carefully afterwards. Making rubbings of different barks will encourage close observation of their colour and texture.

pp. 12–13

Making a musical instrument from a straw is an enjoyable as well as a scientific experience. Experiment by flattening and trimming the sides of the mouthpiece end. Investigate how different sounds are made by varying the position of holes in the straw. Find out if the sound is higher or lower if a hole is made near the open end. Discover what sound is produced if two straws are blown together.

pp. 14–15

If all activity in a wood slows down in Winter, do people slow down, too?

Discuss the changes people make to adapt to Winter, such as changing their clothing, food, activities and hobbies. Investigate clothing suitable for Winter wear. It must be warm, windproof and waterproof. Test different samples of fabric to find which is best for Winter wear.

pp. 16–17

It is easy to find tracks and signs on or near a bird table, when food is placed there regularly. You can sometimes see signs of other animals such as cats there, too. Tracks can also be found in the soft mud at the edge of a stream or river, or round the school pond. Follow the tracks of birds or other animals in the snow on the lawn, or in the school field. Draw a picture and mark the pattern of the movements.

pp. 18–19

Towards the end of Winter, some evidence of plant growth can be found. Look for plants coming up through the snow; notice how the buds are swelling on the trees. Make a chart to show how many different signs of growth are found, where they are found and when.

As the weather becomes warmer and the days lengthen, the rate of growth will increase. Pots of seeds planted in the same way can be placed in different positions (light/dark, hot/cold) to demonstrate different growth patterns.

pp. 20–21

Moss, lichen or algae may be present on a rotting log. Notice how they grow on the log. Consider differences in colour and texture. Discover the different places in which each may be found. Discuss the reasons for this. Is it related to light, temperature or humidity?

pp. 22–23

Explain why animals need to hunt for food in Winter. Talk about the struggle for survival which takes place in a wood. Show children how they can help by feeding birds in Winter. Discover what the birds like to eat. Find out when they like to feed. How often do you need to put out food? What happens on a really cold day? Do they eat more food or stay away altogether?

pp. 24–25

Look for evidence of nut cases wedged into cracks in bark; this is how some birds extract the nuts. If bark has been stripped from young trees or bushes, deer or squirrels are probably nearby. The bones of rabbits and other small mammals may be discovered at the mouth of a fox's earth, although this is more likely in Summer when there are cubs in the earth.

Index